P9-DSZ-254

Marl Welley

GLACIER BAY
NATIONAL PARK

A L A S K A

GLACIER BAY
NATIONAL PARK

A L A S K A

Photos by
Mark Kelley

Text by
Sherry Simpson

Photographer,
Publisher &
Project Editor: Mark Kelley
Writer: Sherry Simpson
Book and Cover Design: Laura Lucas
Assistant to Mark Kelley &
Historical Researcher: Odette Foster
Text Editors: Larry Persily
Tricia Brown
Proofreaders: Mary Bowen
Paula Cadiente
Rick Kiefer
Mary Lou Elton
Printers: Samwha Printing Co.
Seoul, Korea

Single copies of *Glacier Bay National Park: Alaska*
cost $32.95 for a hard cover edition or $22.95 for
paperback plus $5 for shipping. Retail discounts
are available for booksellers.

Mark Kelley can be reached at P.O. Box 20470,
Juneau, AK 99802; by phone at (toll-free)
(888) 933-1993 or (907) 586-1993; by fax at
(907) 586-1201; by email at photos@markkelley.com;
or on the web at www.markkelley.com

Photographs copyright 2000 by Mark Kelley.
No part of this publication may be reproduced,
stored in a retrieval system, or transmitted in any
form or by any means, electronic, mechanical,
photocopying, recording, or otherwise, without
the prior written permission of the publisher.

Printed by Samwha Printing Co., Ltd., Seoul, Korea
Fourteenth soft cover printing and tenth hard cover
printing, December 2010

ISBN 1-880865-18-1 (hard cover)
ISBN 1-880865-19-X (soft cover)
Library of Congress Catalog Card Number 99-96516

BENJAMIN FRANKLIN AWARD

Mark Kelley's Glacier Bay National
Park, Alaska *book won the 2001
Benjamin Franklin Award in the travel-
essay category. The Benjamin Franklin
Awards are sponsored by the Publishers
Marketing Association, and celebrate
excellence in editorial and design for
books published in 2000.*

*Kelley was one of 54 Benjamin Franklin
Award winners among 1,600 entries.
Judges for the Benjamin Franklin
Awards are acquisition librarians,
bookstore buyers, wholesalers and
distributors, reviewers, editors, designers
and artists. The awards were developed
in 1985 by the Publishers Marketing
Association, a non-profit trade
association of 3,400 publishers.*

cover: Margerie Glacier, Tarr Inlet
half-title page: Rainbow over Walker Glacier along Alsek River
title page left: Backpackers hike the beaches of Glacier Bay National Park.
title page right: Arctic tern, Reid Inlet
back cover: Beach surf, Glacier Bay National Park
left: Oystercatcher

TATSHENSHINI-ALSEK
PARK

BRABAZON RANGE

NOVATAK GLACIER

Alsek River

Ninemyleighter Creek

BRITISH COLUMBIA
ALASKA

SAINT

ELIAS

MOUNTAINS

MELBURN GLACIER

ALSEK

RANGE

GRAND PACIFIC GLACIER

TSIRKU GLACIER

Mt.
McDonnell

BRITISH COLUMBIA
ALASKA

Kiehini River

Chilkat River

Skagway

Klukwan

Taiya Inlet

Tsirku River

Taklin River

Haines

TAKHINSHA

MOUNTAINS

Dry Bay

Alsek River

GLACIER BAY
NATIONAL
PRESERVE

ALSEK GLACIER

DECEPTION HILLS

East Alsek R

GRAND PLATEAU GLACIER

Mt.
Lodge

Mt. Root

Mt. Fairweather

Mt. Quincy
Adams

Mt. Salisbury

FAIRWEATHER GLACIER

CAPE
FAIRWEATHER

FAIRWEATHER

RANGE

Lituya
Mountain

Lituya Glacier

Margerie Glacier

Johns Hopkins Glacier

Johns Hopkins Inlet

Mt.
Cooper

Mt. Abbe

Tarr Inlet

Rendu Glacier

Rendu Inlet

CARROLL GLACIER

Cushing Glacier

MUIR GLACIER

Riggs Glacier

Still Glacier

White
Thunder
Ridge

Queen Inlet

Wachusett Inlet

McBride Glacier

Casement Glacier

Davidson Glacier

LYNN CANAL

CANADA

UNITED STATES

RUSSELL
ISLAND

Lamplugh Glacier

Reid Glacier

Muir Inlet

Adams Inlet

MUIR
POINT

Mt.
Wright

GULF OF ALASKA

PACIFIC OCEAN

Lituya Bay

North Crillon Glacier

Mt.
Bertha

Mt.
Crillon

GLACIER BAY
NATIONAL
PARK

Blue Mouse
Cove

Hugh Miller
Inlet

GLACIER

BAY

TLINGIT
POINT

South Sandy
Cove

NORTH
MARBLE
ISLAND

DRAKE
ISLAND

SOUTH
MARBLE
ISLAND

Bartlett River

Beartrack

Excursion River

CHILKAT

RANGE

Crillon Lake

LAPEROUSE GLACIER

Mt.
LaPerouse

BRADY
ICEFIELD

Gelkie Inlet

FRANCIS
ISLAND

WILLOUGHBY
ISLAND

Fingers
Bay

Berg Bay

Beartrack
Cove

BEARDSLEE
ISLANDS

ICY POINT

Palma
Bay

BRADY GLACIER

Dundas River

Dundas
Bay

Visitor Center
Glacier Bay Lodge

Bartlett Cove

Gustavus

PLEASANT
ISLAND

Dixon Harbor

Torch Bay

Graves Harbor

Taylor
Bay

North Passage

LEMESURIER
ISLAND

ICY

STRAIT

CAPE
SPENCER

CROSS SOUND

South Passage

INIAN
ISLANDS

Elfin
Cove

Excursion Inlet

CHICHAGOF ISLAND

Hoonah

ALASKA

Glacier Bay
National Park
& Preserve

North

Glacier Bay
National Park & Preserve
Boundary

0   5   10   15 Kilometers
0   5   10   15 Miles

Johns Hopkins Inlet in early March ▶
White Thunder Ridge, Muir Inlet ▶▶

▲ Sea lions on Graves Rock with Fairweather Range in background
◄ Fairweather Range from Alsek Glacier to Mount Fairweather

Kayaker, Scidmore Bay ▲
Floatplanes load and unload back-to-back trips of
kayakers from the upper reaches of Muir Inlet. ▶

▲ Moonset above Marble Mountain

◄ Crillon Glacier and Crillon Lake

Land of
Contrast

▲ Nanny and baby mountain goat on Gloomy Knob
◄ The Nunatak, Mount Case and Mount Wright, Muir Inlet

LAND OF CONTRAST

Some places in the world fill a space larger than their actual geography. I realized the truth of this as our small plane flew over Glacier Bay on a clear June morning. Below us lay the eternal winter of rumpled icefields. Stony peaks razored the sky, and at their feet the sea stirred against the shore. Sometimes a brilliant detail emerged: the tropical greens of shallow bays scalloping the coastline, or the gash marking a hillside where an alpine lake had burst free and drained in one ferocious surge. It was as if we floated above both the beginning and the end of the world, a world that contained both chaos and serenity.

As the plane crossed over the bay's main inlets, I traced the routes of the few journeys I'd made in this place, trying in one long gaze to complete trips that took days to accomplish. I could see where I had walked a shoreline, or paddled against a tide, or huddled in the rain for an afternoon. What small journeys they were, and yet how immense. From the air, I could see how much lay beyond the tiny slivers of the landscape I'd seen. Surely everyone who travels in Glacier Bay returns longing to see what was in the next cove, or over the next ridge. But nobody can ever know everything about a place like this. Nobody should ever know all of it, because our lives need such mystery and longing.

Visiting here is like opening the back of a pocket watch and realizing how complicated the mechanism is. Things proceed at their own mysterious pace. Glaciers recede and advance. Vegetation forges ahead. Even the ground rises

▲ **Pigeon guillemots, Tarr Inlet**

◄ **Lamplugh Glacier calves.**

measurably each year as it rebounds from the weight of ice that smothered this corner of Southeast Alaska two centuries ago. You can examine each tiny cog and study every subtle ratchet, and still these movements cannot explain the whole laid out before you.

Glacier Bay is not just a place of physical transformation. People can change here, too. They learn to see the world differently, to find beauty not only in serenity but in severity. This happened to me. On my first kayak trip into Glacier Bay, the rain fell for days. It came not in the harmless drizzle that naturalist John Muir described as "of good quality," but in cold, drenching pellets. The wind blew, too. This is a place where a person must expect a certain rawness of landscape and experience, but not everyone can be as cheerful about such things as Muir. So my friend and I sat glumly on a beach near Goose Cove in the East Arm one gray afternoon and waited for the weather to shift. The longer we sat on the beach watching waves slop against the shore, the more I saw. Deep drifts of empty mussel shells glowed in pink and indigo. Beach rye and alder leaves glistened. The milky turquoise of the inlet shimmered. And when a humpback whale suddenly parted the waters before us, the sight of it lifted us to our feet. We had finally glimpsed the true Glacier Bay, where everything can change in a moment.

And when a humpback whale suddenly parted the waters before us, the sight of it lifted us to our feet.

◄ **Humpback whale tail, Icy Strait with Glacier Bay National Park in background**

► **Beach camp along West Arm**

There is grandeur here, but there is also simple grace in the way an oystercatcher turns a crimson-eyed gaze your way.

So many of us come to Glacier Bay to be overwhelmed by mountains, to be dazzled by glaciers, to be thrilled by animals. We want wilderness with a capital W. Instead of sitting quietly and looking carefully, we tend to tally everything we see. What is to be gained in tracking the number of tidewater glaciers admired, the count of eagles sighted, the sum of bears photographed? To mistake enumeration for enlightenment is to have seen nothing at all. In a place calibrated by epic measurements of time — in ice ages, glacial retreats, forest growth—we sometimes ignore the quiet moments unfolding around us. There is grandeur here, but there is also simple grace in the way an oystercatcher turns a crimson-eyed gaze your way. There are natural melodramas throughout the bay, but what could be more astounding than knowing that the feathery bloom of dryas plants on bare ground is really a prophecy of forests to come? And where is the power of crashing icefalls without the vibrating silence afterward?

Every one of us who attempts to capture Glacier Bay fails and always will, because this is a place that cannot be preserved by words or photographs or statistics. Look away, and everything becomes new. The light shifts. The ice cascades. The tide ebbs. Glaciers carve up time and leave behind a stony blank space, and then life fills up the space slowly, slowly. This is the world on its way to becoming something else. This is the world remembering itself.

◄ ◄ **Seaweed and beach greens at Reid Inlet**
◄ **Black oystercatcher**

▲ Pigeon guillemot on iceberg, Tarr Inlet

◀ Kayakers paddle past Riggs Glacier, Muir Inlet.

The Province of Ice

▲ Beached icebergs, Reid Inlet, Reid Glacier

◄ Icebergs, Alsek Lake

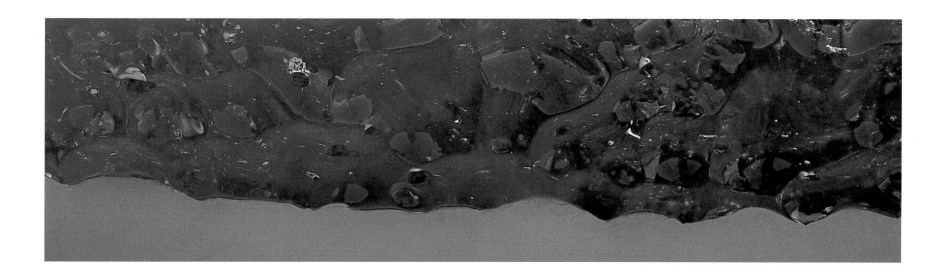

THE PROVINCE OF ICE

For two nights, my husband and I camped on a wedge of rock just around the corner from Lamplugh Glacier. High tide marooned the point from the mainland, making it an island twice a day. We rolled out our sleeping bags on the flattest, highest spot. Scattered across the moss and lichens were crab claws and dry fish bones, the leavings of other creatures that had perched up here, too.

I had never slept in the open before. Rain, mosquitoes, the occasional wild animal wandering past — the slightest threat of these had always pushed me inside some shelter. The stony platform offered no place for a tent, though, and the weather seemed favorable. Sooty clouds loitered a few miles behind us, but above us the sky re-mained clear except for hazy ribbons streaming off the tallest Fairweather peaks.

Far up the gullet of Tarr Inlet, the last rosy glow of the day faded on the bluffs. As the sun glided behind the mountains, the boats skipping around the inlet left, so that a great silence descended as the light failed. Blue shadows crept up from the water and filled the wide basin of Johns Hopkins Inlet. The mountains seemed so astounding in their spare grandeur that every so often we'd have to sit up with our sleeping bags wrapped tight around us and look at them again.

A cold wind flowed off the hidden glacier and over the ridge and across us. The draft pushed mosquitoes away and reminded us that this territory remains always the province of ice.

▲ **Blue iceberg, Alsek Lake**
◄ **Lamplugh Glacier**

⇒ The draft pushed mosquitoes away and reminded us that this territory remains always the province of ice.

The glacier cracked now and then, and once we heard ice cascading hugely into the water. Bergs drifting down from Johns Hopkins stubbled the inlet's smooth sheen. We made a humble fire on slabs of shale, a fire that offered no heat but only a small human comfort in the idea of warmth. I wondered if the seals floating below noticed the orange smudge.

This was a new kind of vulnerability, a way of opening up to the world. Every time I sat up for one more look, I felt the weight of this enormous space pressing on us, and the thought would come again: "No one else here but us." This was true only for a little while, and perhaps it wasn't true at all, but everyone should spend at least one such night in their lives, balancing on the fine edge between fear and exhilaration.

It was almost too much, to have a sky that broad overhead and mountains so weighty bearing down, and the nearby sound of the glacier shifting like an animal. I tried to imagine everything that could go wrong—rolling off the slope into the sea, waking to a bear scrabbling up the knob, and other far-fetched troubles—and then I tried to stop

Kaykers, McBride Glacier, Muir Inlet ▶

The mountains seemed so astounding in their spare grandeur that every so often, we'd have to sit up with our sleeping bags wrapped tight around us and look at them again.

imagining anything at all, but to simply pay attention to what surrounded us. I lay flat against the rock and looked up. A score of seagulls inscribed lazy circles way up high, as if they thought they were eagles rising above the earth. The last thing I saw was the luminous sky above, and midnight stars sparking in the darkest curve of the dome.

In the morning, the pale light poured over us. That's what woke us. An eagle watched the sea from an alder tree on the ridge above. I felt cleansed inside, exactly as if the air had percolated through my lungs and into my blood, seeping through every cell. Nothing had happened to us during the night, and yet everything had. We had slept with the sea rising around us, and a glacial wind flowing across us, and the night sky above us. We had become part of the world completely.

◀ **Moonset over Topeka Glacier, Johns Hopkins Inlet**
▶ **Campfire on beach, West Arm**

33

▲ McBride Glacier, Muir Inlet
▶ Icebergs on beach, McBride Glacier, Muir Inlet

▲ **Alsek Glacier, Alsek Lake**
◄ **River rafters, Alsek River**

"HERE IT IS"

Once a man came all the way from Israel to float down the Tatshenshini River. The Tatshenshini flows from the Yukon watersheds, passing through boreal forests of aspen, birch and spruce, until it joins the Alsek River seventy-seven miles downstream. Together the two waterways create one of the continent's great rivers. Before these commingled rivers pour into the Pacific Ocean, they flow together along the northern edge of Glacier Bay National Park and Preserve.

As with most rivers, the Tatshenshini begins modestly, more like an aggressive stream than a river, and the mountains that surround it are modest as well. For the first few days of the trip, the traveler from Israel took note of the river that was not so big and the mountains that were not so tall. He was not so impressed. Sometimes he remarked that in Israel there are rivers and mountains far more astounding than these. "When will we get to the wilderness?" he asked the river guides. The guides only looked at him and said, "We'll get there. You'll see." He did not appear to believe them.

But as the journey continued, the river grew wider and wilder. The land somehow seemed to open up. Mountains gathered along the horizon, peaks so bold and severe that it seemed the river could not pass through them and surely must run beneath the stone to find the sea. But rivers are more powerful than mountains, and time more powerful still. The river always found a way.

"Here it is." It is the moment when you realize you do not inhabit a place. Instead, the place inhabits you.

▲ **River rafter collects liquid sunshine on sunglasses.**

◄ **Iceberg, Alsek Lake**

One day the man stood looking at the mountains. The river moved so powerfully that large stones rolled and knocked together beneath the silty water's surface. The moon hung over the mountain peaks, almost full, and it seemed as if moon and mountains alike had been carved from the same kind of cold and silvery stone. Surely he thought of other mountains and rivers he had seen in his life. Then he sought out one of the guides who had brought him here. He said, "Here it is." At last he had found what he had come so far to see.

"Here it is." A moment like this can happen to anyone in such a place. I learned this as the river carried us toward Alsek Lake. Rain had pelted us for the past three days, and sometimes it was hard to see beyond the damp chill of our raincoat hoods. But one of the guides started talking about the Tatshenshini-Alsek River, and how he had always wanted to run it, because there was no river like it anywhere. "I loved this river before I knew it," he said.

Looking around with new eyes, I saw what he meant. On the broad plains left by retreating glaciers, wildflowers spread in tidal waves of purples and magentas and yellows. The mountains were so broad and solid that they seemed like immense pillars holding up the clouds. At Alsek Lake, three massive glaciers stair-stepped from the sky, filling the lake with a blue sculpture garden of icebergs. And always the river moved us toward the sea.

"Here it is." It is the moment when you realize you do not inhabit a place. Instead, the place inhabits you.

Field of paintbrush, Alsek River

Iceberg soup, Reid Glacier, West Arm

Where
Spirits
Dwell

▲ Bald eagle
◄ Fairweather Range viewed from Icy Strait.

WHERE SPIRITS DWELL

Few mountains in this world achieve distinction not through size so much as historical and spiritual dimension. Mount Fairweather is one. From the Pacific coast, it seems to emerge directly from the heart of the ocean because the peak lies only 15 miles from the shore. The mountain pinions an entire range along this rim of Alaska, lofting above the other crests at a height of 15,300 feet. Mount Fairweather is the 19th highest peak in North America, but what makes it remarkable is its dramatic lunge skyward at a thousand feet per horizontal mile.

The mountain's prominence and other-worldly aspect has made it a place marker through history. The peak exists in perpetual winter, and this starkness gives it a delicate brilliance against the blue of a cloudless day. Fairweather does not seem to reflect light so much as generate it. In the rosy flood of sunset, it is dream-like. In the clear illumination of mid-day, it becomes coldly radiant. Its bearing is so remarkable that the eye drifts toward it again and again, trying to believe that something so massive yet so ethereal can be more than a mirage.

▲ **Alpenglow on top of Mt. Fairweather**
◄ **Mt. Fairweather from Dry Bay**

"Its appearance gives promise of calm seas or warns of storm, and it is therefore called 'the paddler's mountain'...."

"Its appearance gives promise of calm seas or warns of storm, and it is therefore called 'the paddler's mountain' by the natives," wrote anthropologist Frederica de Laguna. Captain James Cook surely noticed the same effect. He named the peak Fairweather, an appellation also given to the nearby cape and the mountain range draped around the peak. In the mid-18th century, whalers hunting on the Fairweather Grounds used the mountain as a beacon of good weather. Fishermen pitching about on the open ocean have done the same for many years.

The mountain's presence is mythical as well as geological. The peak provided a stone "nest" as a sanctuary against what the Tlingit called the "High Tide All Around," or the Flood, according to de Laguna. One tale regards Fairweather as the wife of the taller Mount St. Elias to the north. When the two quarreled and parted ways, their children, slaves and workers formed the community of mountains around them. The mountain is so powerful that it serves as a clan crest for the Hunas, just as the killer whale, salmon, bear and other living forces of natural history do for other clans.

The western world makes claims to Mount Fairweather in a different way, by laboring upward to stand on the peak's summit. The mountain's architecture is difficult to traverse because glaciers buttress its flanks and colossal icefalls hinder easy approaches. Simply reaching the mountain has always been difficult. Ocean breakers repel climbers hoping to land by boat, and vicious alder thickets make the foothills hellishly frustrating. Mountaineering legend Bradford Washburn described plagues of black flies, treacherous crevasses and backbreaking trudges in an account of his failed attempt in 1930.

"But there isn't a one of us who wouldn't give a fortune to be back again in the shadow of old Fairweather packing in the rain, sleeping on the ice, eating bran flakes and water and playing hide-and-seek with the bears," he concluded.

Mountaineers finally summited the peak in 1931. Their achievement is not necessarily to be envied by those of us bound to the earth's surface. In an account of a later successful climb, Walter Gove and Loren Adkins wrote: "The commanding and impressive view somehow did not compare with the vistas we had had of the rugged mountain on which we now stood."

Simply to gaze upon Mount Fairweather is to believe that spirits do dwell within mountains. ▨

▲ **Female and male willow ptarmigan in spring plumage**
◄ **Sunrise on Mt. Fairweather from Lituya Bay**

L A N D I N M O T I O N

The ground shivered, rocking just enough to wake me in the tent. It was 4:30 a.m., and the thin light was silvery on the water of Johns Hopkins Inlet. Earthquake, I thought dreamily. Most tremors seem like betrayals of gravity as you struggle to keep your balance, but this felt as if a tuning fork had been struck deep in the earth, and the vibrations had rippled from stone through flesh and into my very bones.

I fell asleep again. It was only a minor quake, a 4.3 with an epicenter near Yakutat, about 200 miles away on the outer coast. But that shudder was large enough to shake the illusion that Glacier Bay's underpinnings are permanent. Everything is in motion here, even the land itself.

Occasionally uneasy twitches become violent jerks, rearranging topography. In 1899, a shock near Yakutat knocked about the earth's surface so dramatically that the shoreline jolted upward as much as 47 feet in one spot. The quake agitated Glacier Bay, too. "The glaciers seem to have been completely shattered by the shock," reported Fremont Morse in a 1908 *National Geographic*. Muir Glacier shed so much ice that for several years ships could not come any closer than 10 or 20 miles away.

La Chaussee Spit looking south to Harbor Point, Lituya Bay

Fairweather Range from La Chaussee Spit, Lituya Bay

"At the entrance to this port, twenty-one sailors perished. Whoever you may be, add your tears to ours."

Slabs of the earth's crust jam against each other along this coast, prodding and folding into each other with such power that they forced the Fairweather Range to erupt above the surface. Where the Pacific plate shoves against the North American plate, a wide cleft known as the Fairweather Fault stretches from Icy Point to Yakutat. This earthquake-maker is visible from the air, a warning that Glacier Bay is a place where creation continues, and not always gently.

Nowhere do splendor and cataclysm exist in symmetry as they do in Lituya Bay. In 1786, the French explorer La Perouse described the T-shaped bay as "perhaps the most extraordinary place on earth." The embayment's location makes it the single true shelter along the Fairweather Grounds—but only if mariners approach cautiously, and only if the periodic giant waves that scour the bay hold off for one more day.

La Perouse sailed away in sorrow from this place after two of his longboats were lost to the treacherous La Chaussee Spit at the bay's entrance. One of La Perouse's men composed a message to leave behind on the island he named Cenotaph: "At the entrance to this port, twenty-one sailors perished. Whoever you may be, add your tears to ours." The memorial became prophetic.

Sunset in front of La Chaussee Spit, Lituya Bay ▶

▲ **Tufted puffins**

▶ The scar left by the 1958 landslide-created wave is still visible over 40 years later. The wave scoured away trees along the mountainside to a height of 1,720 feet. To locate the scar as photographed in 1998, look at the tree line in the back lefthand side of Lituya Bay.

The Tlingit understood that the bar was passable only at slack tide, but even they lost canoes there. More tellingly, they spoke of a "monster of the deep" named Kah Lituya who destroyed interlopers in Lituya Bay by shaking the bay's surface like a sheet to create deadly waves.

Modern fishermen may not know of Kah Lituya, but they do understand its power. At sunset on July 9, 1958, the Fairweather Fault slipped dramatically, causing a great earthquake that dislodged a massive slab of earth and trees into the bay. The subsequent splash surged up the opposite hillside, scouring away trees to a height of 1,720 feet. The face of Lituya Glacier crumbled. Within three minutes, the first wave approached three trolling boats anchored near the bay's entrance. The *Edrie*, occupied by Howard Ulrich and his seven-year-old son, rose safely with the wave after its anchor line snapped. Bill and Vi Swanson's boat, the *Badger*, wildly surfed the water stern first across the La Chaussee Spit, rising so high that they looked down from a height of about 80 feet above the trees.

"It felt like we were in a tin can and somebody was shaking it," Bill said later. The boat struck bottom and then foundered offshore, where fishermen rescued the couple. The wave engulfed the *Sunmore*, killing owners Mickey and Orville Wagner.

A calamitous wave also had crashed through the bay in 1936, and geologist Don Miller later concluded that giant waves had occurred in about 1853-54, in 1874, and possibly in 1899. Though he ruled out an earthquake in the 1936 wave, he could not definitely establish its cause. Simply put, he warned that a combination of factors make Lituya Bay especially susceptible to enormously destructive waves.

Fly over Lituya Bay today, and it's possible to distinguish the new growth that has appeared since 1958. Uprooted trees still litter beaches along the coast. And yet, the mountains seem unshakable, the glaciers affixed permanently to the land. A group of sea otters float peaceably on the south side of Cenotaph Island. The beauty here is unreal, intense and edgy. The sun and serenity are not enough to overcome the knowledge that destruction and sorrow have filled this bay before, and surely will again.

Animals of
Glacier Bay

▲ Eagle feather and brown bear print in sand
◄ Brown bear, Blue Mouse Cove

TIMING & LUCK

▲ **Harbor seal mother and pup on iceberg, Johns Hopkins Inlet**

◄ **Hoary marmot, Dundas Bay**

All night long the whales swam back and forth along the shore near York Creek, rising to deliver long, shuddering breaths. In the dreamy twilight the sound seemed to rise all around, so that even our tent walls seemed to billow and flutter with the exhalation of whales. None of us slept well. "There are worse things than to be kept awake by whales," a companion remarked the next morning.

The mountains you can count on. You can pretend the glaciers will always be there. The ocean seems eternal. But the animals surprise you in fleeting moments, emerging from the forest, or flying over in a tremor of wings, or swimming by barely glimpsed. You may come on them suddenly.

You may never come upon them at all. Every animal you see is a miracle of timing and luck.

Often animals are unseen but still part of a landscape of sound, like the keening loons tucked somewhere in the sea's swell, or the winter wrens whistling in the alder brush. But sometimes they watch as you go by. The eagle winging overhead angles its head slightly to cast down a fierce eye. Harbor seals rise silently from the water with an up-periscope motion, their liquid gaze taking you in before they slip below the surface. Ravens shower you with rude comments.

Usually we see only where animals have been. There is a brown bear that spends a lot of time on a knoll above Alsek Lake, along the park's

In the dreamy twilight, the sound seemed to rise all around, so that even our tent walls seemed to billow and flutter with the exhalation of whales.

northern edge. The soil is potholed where the bear has excavated roots with its great shoveling paws. In some places it has scraped shallow beds in which to lie. Imagine that bear snoozing up on that hill, high above giant icebergs drifting in the lake.

Once in a while, an animal happens upon you and stays to see what happens. A black bear grazing along the tideline of Hutchins Bay did not see our group for the longest time, and it was not alarmed when finally it did notice our presence. For an hour or so, it hung around camp, causing a certain amount of consternation. The bear popped its head out of the trees for a sidelong look at us. It loitered in a meadow and chewed grass. It refused to be insulted by our shouts and arm-waving.

I thought it a shamelessly bold bear until I heard a seal researcher remark that she had heard of two incidents where wolves padded into people's camps. The wolves sat down and gazed around with what seemed like curiosity. "Couldn't that black bear simply have been interested in us?" she asked. Yes,

◄ **Humpback whales lunge feed.**

> *You may come upon them suddenly. You may never come upon them at all. Every animal you see is a mixture of timing and luck.*

▲ A pod of sea otters
◄ Bald eagle on iceberg

I thought. We are always photographing and studying and spying on animals, just to see what we can see. Why wouldn't a bear or a wolf or a seal be curious, too?

Sometimes the creatures of Glacier Bay are simply traveling through the territory, like you. I saw a black bear moving quickly along the rocky foot of Mount Wright once. It placed each paw steadily and deliberately among the cobbles that lined the shore, never looking up at our passing kayaks. That was a bear with some place to go. Species survive because individuals such as that bear are always in motion, searching for places to eat,

sleep, hide, find mates, colonize. Glacier Bay is perpetually being rediscovered and reinvaded by all kinds of animals and plants moving into newly deglaciated areas. They are on a journey of generations. Sea otters, reintroduced to nearby waters in 1968, spread slowly into the bay. Salmon nose their way into new streams to spawn. Wolves pass through raw territory until habitats fill in and encourage wanderers to stay longer and longer. Moose follow the alder growth up the inlets. A few decades ago, there were no moose here. The bears are just now figuring out that they are good to eat.

To see any wild animal is to remember that in places like Glacier Bay, almost everything that happens takes place beyond our sight. Late one June night, when a mist blurred the edges of the world, a friend and I followed wolf tracks along the muddy shore. All we could hear was our own footsteps and the sound of waves. The tracks were so fresh and so steady that we walked and walked, hoping that if we followed long enough we would catch up to the wolf itself as it paced along the sea. But that was a distance we could never cross.

Moose, Bartlett Cove ▲
Mountain goat, Gloomy Knob ▶

▲ Mother harbor seal and pup, Johns Hopkins Inlet

◄ Killer whales, Icy Strait with Glacier Bay in background

Identifying Bears

Both brown and black bears walk the shores of Glacier Bay, emerging from the new forests or the hills to search the tidelands for food. Distinguishing between the two species can be difficult sometimes, although it helps to remember that black bears are more common in the lower bay, and brown bears in the upper regions. Pelts are no help. Brown bears are not necessarily brown, nor are black bears exclusively black. Both species also have fur in rich shades of mocha, red, black and blonde.

Facial features provide more reliable clues. Brown bears have a broader head with a "dish face." Black bears have a narrow face defined by a tapered, brown nose. To identify a brown bear, look for the characteristic shoulder hump, which is composed of fat and muscle. With any luck, you won't have the opportunity to notice the brown bear's especially long claws. Adult brown bears grow to a larger size than adult black bears, but a young brown bear might not appear especially large — yet.

Brown bear, Blue Mouse Cove
Black bear eats beach sedges along tideline.

Glacier Bears

A "glacier bear" is the rarest sighting of all. These are black bears with a genetic variation that gives their fur the frosty sheen of ice and clouds. They are hardly ever spotted outside of the Yakutat and Glacier Bay area. Seeing one of these bears has long been noteworthy. Lt. Charles Erskine Wood, who was the uncredited first Western discoverer of Glacier Bay, wrote about such a sighting when he was hunting near Mount Fairweather in 1877:

"We found a bear that, so far as I know, is peculiar to this country. It is a beautiful bluish under color, with the tips of the long hairs silvery white. The traders call it 'St. Elias' silver bear.' "

It seems right that a place like Glacier Bay should be home to a bear the very color of glaciers themselves.

▲ **Glacier bear**
▼ **Black bear stands next to glacier bear.**
▶ **Black bear wanders tidal plain in Glacier Bay National Park.**

Marble Islands

The Marble Islands are as densely packed with life — squawking, heaving, fluttering life—as tiny planets floating in their own universe. People are the satellites here, circling in boats just close enough to witness the commotion of birds and creatures. The islands are reliable places to see two of Glacier Bay's main attractions: sea lions and puffins. Completely opposite to their balletic manner in the water, scores of sea lions wallow around this haul-out like sumo wrestlers. The largest seabird colonies in the bay claim these islands, too. The exotics are the horned and tufted puffins, which breed here despite being an oceangoing sort. Nesting horned puffins wedge themselves into fissures and shallow hollows, and tufted puffins tunnel deeper into the earth. To see them fly through the air is to appreciate the frivolous side of nature; to witness them flying underwater is to understand the true meaning of grace.

▲ **Sea lions haul out on South Marble Island.**
◄ **Seagulls circle above the South Marble Island.**

Birds of
Glacier Bay

▲ Seagull and bald eagle, McBride Glacier
◄ Hike along Glacier Bay National Park beach

BIRDS OF GLACIER BAY

very spring the Earth inclines, and birds pour across the sky into Glacier Bay. The list of species stretches well beyond two hundred. Among them are birds of the sea, the forest, the shore, the meadow, the tundra, the cliffs. There are divers, swoopers, singers, beach-pickers, gliders, surfers. Some cannot be ignored, and others are rarely glimpsed. Think of how the bald eagle dominates the air with a grand flap of wings, and of how the rufous hummingbird disappears into it, nothing more than buzz and flash.

Glacier Bay appeals to so many kinds of birds because so many kinds of habitat exist here. Species that might otherwise persevere onward

to arctic plains can find similar places here where vegetation is still reclaiming newly glaciated terrain. The Pacific flyway, a major migratory artery, pulses above the coast, and at least 65 species of seabirds migrate or breed along this stretch. Geese, ducks and other long-distance travelers often pause on their annual drifts north and south.

Some migrants are among the world's great pilgrims. Red-necked phalaropes, one of the most populous species in late summer, shuttle back and forth from South America. Arctic terns rudder through the air on forked tails and sharp wings just to come here and nest on the barest ground. You will know when you near its speckled eggs

▲ **Cormorant, Tarr Inlet**
◄ **Arctic tern on iceberg, Reid Inlet**

▲ **Jaeger, Dry Bay**
► **Paintbrush in a
field of beach pea,
Dry Bay**

because the tern is a relentless defender that dive-bombs intruders until they retreat, cowed by a creature barely over a foot long. By the time the tern family returns to South American and Antarctic waters, they will have flown 20,000 miles or more.

The point of all this is the oldest story in the world: reproduction of species. Some birds depend less on fierceness and more on fraud to defend their nests. The black oystercatcher, one of the most distinctive shorebirds, is comically transparent in its efforts to draw away predators who might stumble upon its eggs lying unsheltered on gravel beaches. Bobbing its red bill like a lure and stalking away, it settles on invisible eggs in a melodramatic fakery. The tide is one of its many enemies, though, sometimes creeping upon the nest when the eggs have been deposited too close to the water.

Other birds have no need for elaborate ruses. They nest in the tops of trees, like the mysterious marbled murrelet, or in cliff-side condominiums, like herring gulls, black-legged kittiwakes, pigeon guillemots and pelagic cormorants. Kittlitz's murrelets are so reclusive that only a handful of nests have been discovered, all of them in Alaska.

Glacier Bay is riddled with such hide-outs. Molting geese and ducks seclude

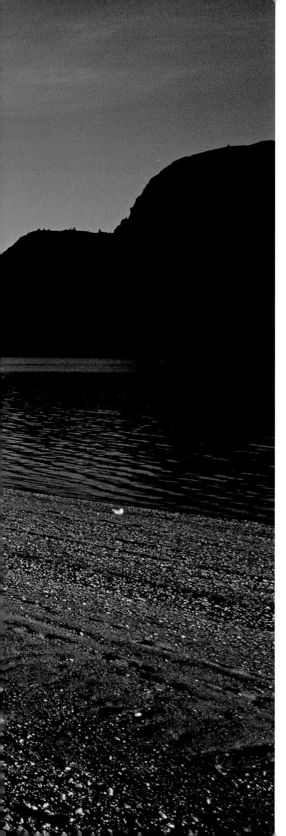

themselves in estuaries and on islands, hoping their feathers arrive before their predators. Varied thrushes are nearly impossible to spot in mature forests, but their melancholy chimes echo through the trees. Ptarmigan cackle, blue grouse hoot, sparrows trill their refrains again and again. This is how we know some birds best, by the layers of sound wafting through the bay.

Other birds you could not avoid if you tried. Scoters, white-winged and surf, skip across the waves and gather companionably in huge rafts. Common murres are, well, the most common species, with more than 15,000 of them lingering through winter. Herring and glaucous-winged gulls barely draw an interested glance, they seem so familiar, but they claim a natural history as convoluted as any.

So many other species live here in an amazing range of behavior, coloration, life history. There are birds of startling plumage and birds as plain as cardboard, birds that launch themselves on heroic journeys and birds that remain through every season. Of all the places in the world, they choose this place, often year after year, and that itself is the most remarkable thing: the fidelity of birds. 〽

▲ **Black oystercatcher sits on beach nest just above the high tide line mark.**

◀ **Beach along Muir Inlet**

▲ Western sandpiper, Reid Inlet
◄ Flock of knots, Reid Inlet

Kittiwakes

On the cliffs beside Margerie Glacier, almost 3,000 pairs of black-legged kittiwakes build nests and feed on krill and small fish. The constant sound and motion of these long-lived gulls mask a worrisome scientific puzzle: Why is the colony failing to breed successfully? This colony, the largest and most studied in the bay, may produce fewer than one hundred chicks in a year. Because the nests are difficult to observe, researchers can't tell if the birds aren't laying eggs, if eggs aren't hatching, or if chicks are starving. Inadequate food could factor into any of these scenarios. Between 4 million and 10 million black-legged kittiwakes live in Alaska, but population declines and breeding failures have been common throughout the North Pacific during the past quarter-century, making kittiwake research even more important here.

▲ **Black-legged kittiwakes fly off their nests at their colony next to Margerie Glacier.**

◀ **Black-legged kittiwakes on their nests, Margerie Glacier**

Succession

▲ Bear bread and dwarf dogwood, Bartlett Cove
◄ False lily-of-the-valley along the forest edge of Bartlett Cove

▲ **Dryas flowers, Muir Inlet**
◀ **Dryas goes to seed along Muir Inlet.**

S U C C E S S I O N

I t's a modest plant, this conquerer of continents, but *Dryas drummondi* has helped transform North America and Europe since the last Ice Age. Also known as mountain avens, the flower's yellow twist is easy to overlook among the more exalted wonders of Glacier Bay. But, this remarkable organism is one of the keys to a critical scientific problem: Bare soil can't hold water or nutrients, so exactly how does ground scoured by glaciers become transformed into forests?

This ecological alchemy is performed by plants like dryas in a process known as primary succession. The mechanisms of succession have intrigued scientists for decades, making Glacier Bay an "unexcelled laboratory for testing ideas about how landscape becomes clothed with organisms and how the soil develops after the melting of continental ice sheets," according to Donald Lawrence, one of the foremost scientists to spend time in this classy laboratory.

Until recently, succession seemed pretty straightforward. Most visitors understand that Glacier Bay offers a wonderful illustration of the process, with barren glaciated rock as Exhibit A and forested Bartlett Cove as Exhibit B, 225 years after glaciers departed. Here is the simplistic description of succession:

◀ **Devils club grows in the mature forest along Bartlett River.**

▶ **Backpackers travel along a bear trail just inside the forest fringe by Lituya Bay.**

⧉ The forest matures as spruce stands mix with western hemlock, creating the luxuriantly green chapels of light.

After ice recedes, leaving a rubble of silt and stone, lichens and mosses break down the soil. Then pioneering plants such as dryas, fireweed, alder and Indian paintbrush appear and help create organic soil. Dryas and alder perform a critical step by sucking nitrogen from the air (with the help of micro-organisms) and making it available to other plants that need nitrogen to thrive.

Alder thickets follow with a vengeance, seemingly bent on world domination. Eventually, after helping to fertilize the soil, they give way to other shrubs and trees, including willows, cottonwoods and Sitka spruce trees. The forest matures as spruce stands mix with western hemlock, creating the luxuriantly green chapels of light we associate with Bartlett Cove. Muskeg is the endgame.

The entire sequence seems as orderly as a recipe: just add nitrogen and water, and voilá, a forest emerges. But scientists have realized that succession is marvelously complicated (and therefore, marvelously interesting). For example, alder thickets never grew in some older parts of the lower bay. It turns out that many factors influence which plants germinate where, how quickly they grow, and how much they help and hinder the growth of other plants. Nothing is as simple as it seems. That's why Glacier Bay will continue to act as an "unexcelled laboratory" for further generations of scientists teasing apart this puzzle.

In the meantime, glaciers keep receding and dryas continues laboring to change the very earth. The flower's yellow twist mellows into a lion's mane of seeds, the silvery-green leaves expand in thick cushions, and the roots grab more tightly to the ground. One dryas plant grows almost exponentially within a few years into a lush, matted disc. Mats that are two decades old can average 18 feet in diameter. Eventually these small galaxies of dryas join, cloaking the ground in green and gold and claiming yet more scrap of the continent. ▨

▲ Lesser yellowlegs cries out from its perch in
the top of spruce tree in Dry Bay.

◀ Spruce tree drips with spruce cones.

▲ Alder leaves bud in spring.

▶ Skunk cabbage is not located in the bay proper but on the outer coastal areas and around Excursion Inlet.

▶▶ Fiddleheads spring up along forest in Bartlett Cove.

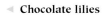 Chocolate lilies
 Salmonberry flowers
▶ Paintbrush and lupine, Bartlett Cove

▶ **Blue grouse on the forest floor, Bartlett Cove**

◀ **Club moss, Bartlett Cove**

People

▲ Nathan Schroeder with his dungeness crab catch

◄ Mount Fairweather Dancers from Hoonah

H O O N A H

▲ Mount Fairweather Dancers dressed in traditional regalia perform on stage at *Celebration '98*.

◄ The Tlingit village of Hoonah is located on Chichagof Island across from Glacier Bay.

In some libraries there is a thin booklet titled *Glacier Bay History*. The original title is *Sít' K̲aa Káx̲ Kana.áa*. Open the pages hoping to understand the region's past and you will discover that every word is in the Tlingit language. This is how the history begins, as translated from the words of Huna Tlingit spokeswoman Susie James: "G̲at Héenee yóo áwe duwasáakw wé haa aanée G̲at Héenee." "The name of it is Gatheeni, that land of ours."

The words are not our words. The language is not our language. The history is not our history.

Even in translation, the subtle meanings and emotions of this story lie beyond our understanding. To hold this slim book is to realize the distance between Glacier Bay as a place to visit for a few days and Glacier Bay as the spiritual and sustaining core of a culture.

"All our stories, our songs, our names, and our regalia have their origins from our homeland, which is Glacier Bay," says Kenneth Grant, president of the Hoonah Indian Association. Grant, whose Tlingit name is X̲oolx̲aa, is a Raven and a member of the T'ak̲deintaan clan. He notes that it is impossible to talk about Glacier Bay in the present without talking about the past. "The connection is very strong today. All of our rituals that we have began in Glacier Bay. The food-gathering, the hunting, a lot of our spiritual ceremonies come from Glacier Bay."

The Tlingit, one of Alaska's major indigenous peoples, live throughout Southeast Alaska. The Huna Tlingit lived not only in Glacier Bay but at sites along Icy Strait and as far north as Lituya Bay. Other groups once lived around the Alsek River, near the park's northern boundary, but the Hunas are the predominant people of the Glacier Bay region. The Tlingit people divided their territory into areas known as "kwáans," which means "people of that place." The contemporary home of the X̲una K̲'aa woo is the village of Hoonah on Chichagof Island. Tlingits identify themselves in many ways through a complicated social structure that includes families, or clans. Two Huna clans in particular are identified with Glacier Bay, the Chookaneidí and the T'ak̲deintaan.

The Octopus trail marker carved by Rick Beasley marks the traditional settlement area of the Eagle moiety Chookaneidí (Brown Bear) clan in Bartlett Cove.

The restless advance and retreat of ice over the centuries, as well as the rebounding land and shifting shorelines, makes it difficult to establish firm timelines and patterns of humans here. Evidence of prehistoric occupation in the region dates to at least 9,000 years ago. Huna accounts mention places, events and customs that occurred before the last glaciation of a few hundred years ago. Villages, homes and camps were overtaken by the ice, leaving little evidence. However, here and there archaeological surveys have discovered artifacts from ancient summer camps, the location of a settlement called Hooknoowoo, or Dry Fort, and other evidence consonant with Tlingit remembrances of events and life here.

Nearly everything else known comes from the words of the Tlingit themselves. In Glacier Bay, the real names are those of the people who once lived here and regard it as their country still. Many names describe not only specific sites, but motion and event and myth. Hugh Miller Inlet is actually "Where the Glacier Ice Broke Through." Johns Hopkins Inlet is "The Inlet that Broke Towards Behind Mount Fairweather." A spot on the Alsek River is "Place Where Raven Wiped His Beak."

There is more to know here, in tales, songs and memories that signify more than colorful legends spun out for entertainment. "I know a lot of times our stories and everything that intertwines seems like folklore — but for us it's our history," said Mary Rudolph, whose Tlingit name is Jina haag.

In her story, Chookaneidí elder Susie James tells of a time when five separate house groups lived in the bay. Her story is complemented by a similar version told by Chookaneidí matriarch Amy Marvin. Both stories refer to a tragic event caused when a bored teenage girl called down the glacier's spirit, forcing the people to flee. Though slightly different in detail, each story is pervaded by a sense of loss. In one version, the girl stays behind and sacrifices herself, and in the other the girl's grandmother takes her place. The bereft people resettled beyond the ice in several nearby places. Eventually they gathered in the village known as Hoonah.

Today, the park boundaries seem artificial to a people who still define their lives not by lines on a map but by the arc of seasons. This region has always offered seal, fish, berries, bird eggs, greens, meat and fur, but Glacier Bay represents far more than a natural larder. It is tied in an inexplicable, essential way to what it means to be a Huna Tlingit. Old symbols of that connection still exist on several coastal mountains high above the water, beyond the reach of ice. Cairns placed there long ago signal that, to the Tlingit, this place is not a wilderness, not a recreational destination, not a tourist attraction.

"All of Glacier Bay is a treasure," elder Wilbur James, or Shadahéix, explained to the scientists. "There is no one who loves and values his homeland more than a Tlingit. We are very proud of this, our home."

Note: Some quotes and some information here appeared first in *Proceedings of the Third Glacier Bay Science Symposium, 1993* published by the National Park Service in 1995. Complete translations of the history of Glacier Bay as related by Amy Marvin and Susie James can be found in *Haa Shuká, Our Ancestors: Tlingit Oral Narratives*, edited by Nora Marks Dauenhauer and Richard Dauenhauer, published in 1987 by University of Washington Press and Sealaska Heritage Foundation.

G U S T A V U S

▲ **Gustavus beach front with Beartrack Mountains in background**

It's not easy locating Gustavus. The town is on the map, all right, just around the corner from Glacier Bay on that broad plain edging Icy Strait. Once there, you can identify the kinds of buildings a proper town of 400 should have: a post office, a library, a school. There are even a few features most Alaska towns don't enjoy. (A golf course? Out here in the middle of wilderness?) But there is no downtown, no streets neatly lined with houses, no main square. Instead, you'll find homes and a few businesses scattered throughout green meadows and dark forest.

The true Gustavus is not a physical place so much as chain of actions, conversations, choices about how best to live. If you walk around looking for Gustavus, your arm will grow weary from waving at everybody who waves at you. (If you live here and fail to wave back, I was told, folks will wonder what's wrong with you.) This is a place where people talk to each other. And talk. And talk. There's no such thing as a short trip to the dock, the airport, the store. At the mercantile, a neighbor tells another about the black bear loitering in the compost heap. Parking lot philosophers lean on their pickup trucks and wonder how to keep Gustavus so . . . Gustavus. There's no such thing as a private table at the Strawberry Point Cafe.

Even the homes are saying something. No house is like any other, each reflecting somebody's personal idiosyncracies and outlook.

▲ Adrienne Bosworth pumps a glass of water from her kitchen sink faucet.
▶ Bosworth homestead off Tong Road, Gustavus

A first-rate home here is not defined by square footage or the size of the garage, but by whether it has a finely crafted outhouse, a sauna big enough for the neighbors, a productive garden, an inspiring view, a trouble-free rainwater cistern. An attractive real estate perk might be a meandering creek or an especially good strawberry patch.

With all of this free expression running rampant, Gustavus is also a place where people argue a lot—civilly, of course. Is it time for a formal government yet? (Voters recently turned down incorporation by two votes.) Should tourism be encouraged to nurture the slow-motion economy, or discouraged to preserve small-town life? Should the town build a real dock, or should it always be just a little difficult to come here?

The trouble is that it's too easy to fall in love with Gustavus. Once while crossing the Salmon River Bridge, I met a teenage boy with a golden retriever, a fishing rod and a bicycle. His cheeks were flushed, his smile wide, and he held up a stringer of three silvery Dolly Vardens for my admiration. Can a place this charming be for real? Even Norman Rockwell might think he'd gone over the top with such a wholesome scene.

"How many places in the world do you think you can call someone by their first name in a newspaper and have the entire town know whom you are referring to?" wrote

a homesick college student to the local newspaper, *Icy Passages.* I read that and thought, "How many places in the world do you think college students write letters to their community saying they are homesick?"

When people aren't talking, they're writing messages to each other on bulletin boards. There's a yurt warming, and everyone's invited. Needed, some kind of job. If you spot some orcas from your boat, could you let the killer whale biologist know? Does anyone have a horse that a seven-year-old could ride occasionally? The writing group is meeting Saturday. Oh yes, it's time to start planning the famous Gustavus Fourth of July—volun-

teers are needed to organize the parade, set up the kid's three-legged race and arrange Chicken Poop Bingo.

A post office poet tacks a handmade card on the wall: "May the beauty and mystery that surrounds you find its way into your heart." This is a reminder that Gustavus is a good place to find quiet, too. On a clear day the Fairweather Range materializes on the horizon like a magician's illusion. Meadows purpled with iris and fireweed ease into forest, all of it reclaimed from glaciers. People live cheek-by-jowl with the wilderness that could not be banished by the homesteaders who settled here early in the century to raise

◀ **Restored working 1930s gas pumps grace the town's only gas station.**
▶ **Gustavus viewed from just past the boat harbor along the Salmon River.**

cattle and crops. There's seaweed to sweeten garden soil, fish to catch, wild strawberries to pick, vegetables to harvest. Moose, bears, wolves—they all live here, too.

"It appeals to people who want the country life yet," says Doris Howe, who has lived here for many years with her husband, Bob.

Gustavus is too sophisticated to be merely quaint, though. The residents aren't recluses who couldn't survive in the real world. (Well, most aren't, anyway.) They are fishermen, National Park Service employees, retirees, descendants of pioneers, innkeepers, writers, artists, naturalists, backcountry guides and thinkers. They are smart, engaged people who want to live the way they choose in a place "where the safest thing to do with your car keys is to spot weld them to the ignition so you don't lose them," one resident wrote.

People do for themselves here, and they do for each other. "You have to be on good terms with your neighbors," says Rita Wilson, a woman of startling energy. "We're too dependent on each other." Gustavus residents like to point out the good things "other" people do. Rita was short 75 cents at the post office one day and three people offered to pay for her. Mary Hervin mends clothes for busy mothers and seeds her trademark pink lupine throughout town. Sally Lesh told youngsters she'd show them how to knit, and Jack Lesh has been teaching Spanish. One summer, more than 30 people volunteered to read books with children.

Probably there is more initiative and volunteerism here per square inch than anywhere else in Alaska. A Park Service ranger is also a minister; a therapist does carpentry and small jobs, too. Paul Berry is the most enthusiastic "dumpmaster" in the world, people say, and because of him and others, Gustavus' landfill has a successful recycling program. (Thank him with chocolate and flowers, someone urged in the newspaper.) Folks raised more than $20,000 to help build a new public library, not including smaller labors of love. The town paid to send the clinic's physician's assistant to the Lower 48 for training. And people built a house for a local single mother so she wouldn't have to leave.

"Everybody's so good to you here," says Mary Hervin, herself one of the town's chief do-gooders.

Not that there aren't problems. Most are caused by Gustavus' position as a gateway to a popular national park. Some people consider that providential, and some a plague, but the result is that every year more people stop here permanently once they pass through the gate. Every summer the population doubles. Until recently, there was no electricity, television or paved roads. Now Gustavus is an easier place to live, and an easier place to make a living, and not every face is familiar anymore.

"It's an important time for Gustavus," says Bruce Paige, president of the Gustavus Community Association, a nonprofit organization that runs municipal affairs. "But it's not easy."

Gustavus is too beautiful to believe, too important to lose. There aren't many places like it left in the world. The people who live here know that better than any of us.

"Gustavus is changing, but it's still better than the next best place," says Bob Howe, a former superintendent of Glacier Bay National Monument and one of those who came decades ago and discovered his true home. Then he puts on his hat and goes to check on an old friend, same as he does every morning he's in town. And Mary Hervin looks out her window at the hundred-foot patch of pink lupine in her yard and says something that sounds like a small prayer: "We just hope our community holds together right."

"You play this course and look at the scenery—there's not a course in the world that will rival the scenery there."

▲ **Owner of the Mt. Fairweather Golf Course, Morgan DeBoer, putts
the green on Hole #5 with the Fairweather Range as a backdrop.**

▲ Southeast Alaska golf shoes
▶ With his dog in step, Joe Sargent bikes with his clubs over his shoulder for a round of golf.

Mount Fairweather Golf Course

People come to Gustavus to fish, watch whales and admire the splendors of Glacier Bay. They go to Palm Beach to golf. So the sight of the Mount Fairweather Golf Course is a little surprising. Since owner Morgan DeBoer developed the nine-hole course on his lush tidal meadowlands, the course has developed a devout following among locals and visitors. Created on the same principles as links in Scotland, with legitimate greens and challenging shots, this is a course like no other in the world. Players take a break by munching on wild strawberries.

Rule No. 4, "Take Relief From Moose Tracks," gives golfers permission to nudge balls out of hoof prints. Any eagles are likely to be bald. Golfers play around geese, and ravens are known to steal range balls. The nearby beach is referred to as the "world's biggest sand trap," and high tide produces a natural water hazard near Holes 3, 4 and 5. "Nice part is you can get your ball back when the tide goes out," DeBoer says.

This is a purely Alaska course, where rubber boots replace golf shoes and plastic drainpipe can serve as a golf bag. Players leave their fees in a plastic coffee can with a hole poked through the lid. DeBoer, the descendant of a local pioneering family, developed the course as a way of protecting his inheritance from development. Though these links may never appear on a pro tour, the views of Mount Fairweather and Icy Strait create their own kind of trophy play. As local golfer Dick Levitt says, "You play this course and look at the scenery—there's not a course in the world that will rival the scenery there."

"R E F U G I A"

Few places escaped the last big Ice Age in Glacier Bay and survived as islands of life amid a frozen sea. These ancient ecosystems still exist on the tops of some mountains and in places along the coast. They are known as "refugia."

Glacier Bay itself is a refugia for so many of us, a place that seems safe from the creep of civilization. Here we can return briefly to a time that doesn't exist anywhere else. We can encounter nature on its own terms. We can surrender to tides and weather and chance. We can be surprised by the world again.

Everyone wants something different from Glacier Bay: scenery; the chance to gaze at whales, bears and ice; the opportunity to remember what wilderness is like. Most of us crave what Eliza Scidmore felt when she came here in 1883: "the consciousness that so few had ever gazed upon the scene before us, and there were neither guides nor guide books to tell us which way to go, and what emotions to feel."

To discover Glacier Bay anew—that's what we all want, of course. The danger is that so many of us want this that we risk turning the park into a commodity, a "wilderness experience" of the falsest kind. A few years ago, readers of *Consumer Reports* magazine rated Glacier Bay National Park and Preserve as the best in the country. That such a rating even exists means that every year more and more of us will want to come to such an amazing place, and to come on our own terms, and

Here we can return briefly to a time that doesn't exist anywhere else.

then . . . well, it is the same old story. You can witness the results almost anywhere.

How many of us is too many? That's a question worth asking because every person who enters this landscape alters it somehow. As one guide says, "There's no such thing as no impact."

It is not in our nature to turn away from such places. What's difficult to relinquish is not merely the feeling that we have a right to be here, but the simple and powerful desire to be here. Because of course we do belong in places like Glacier Bay. To say otherwise is to deny that we have any place in the world at all. The problem is not whether we should be here, but how to be here.

Let us refrain from reducing Glacier Bay to a mere piece of scenery. Let us see it for what it is: a landscape unto itself, where life stands for nothing but itself. Let us understand that among all that is mighty—the grinding glaciers, the unstoppable tides, the rising earth — we ourselves have become the most intense force of irreversible change in Glacier Bay.

▲ **Sunset, Dry Bay**
◀ **Sunset from Cape Spencer**

▲ Cruise ship in front of Margerie Glacier, Tarr Inlet

A Timeline of Human History in Glacier Bay National Park and Preserve

Compiled by Odette Foster

▲ **Photographer at Muir Glacier, 1895**　　GBNP #5303

Village of Tuxshecan, Bartlett Cove, c.1891
AMNH #41619

Hoonah Tlingits, 1907
ASL PCA 01-4193

Petroglyphs mark the boundaries of clan holdings.
ASL PCA 01-4184

Captain James Cook ASL PCA 20-243

900-1400 AD • Tlingit Indians and their ancestors inhabit much of what is now Glacier Bay National Park and Preserve, with both permanent and seasonal settlements. Food and other resources are abundant. The Tlingits thrive and develop a culture rich in woodworking, weaving, oratory, dance, trade and warfare.

Sometime after 1500 AD • The advancing glaciers of the Little Ice Age force the Tlingit people to abandon their village at Bartlett Cove. Tlingit oral tradition recounts how the girl, Kaasteen, while secluded during her three-year training as a woman, calls out to a distant glacier. By addressing the ice spirit directly and by failing to exercise self control, she violates two taboos. Her foolish behavior has disastrous consequences. The glacier rapidly advances and destroys the village's long houses. As the villagers evacuate their families by canoe, Kaasteen chooses to stay behind, sacrificing her life to atone for her grave mistake. Her spirit is trapped in the ice. Two of the Chookaneidí clan's most sacred songs mourn the loss of the young woman and her unborn children, the destruction of their homes and belongings, and the hardship of starting over in a new place. (In another Tlingit version of the story, Kaasteen's grandmother chooses to make the sacrifice.) The clans eventually settle in Hoonah, on the south shore of Icy Strait.

As the ice retreats, the Tlingits use permanent and seasonal sites in Glacier and Lituya Bays as their "breadbasket," to hunt and fish, maintain trap lines and smokehouses, collect gull eggs, berries and seaweed. They call the area Sitadaka, and the word survives in the name of Sitakaday Narrows, at the mouth of the bay.

1742-1780s • Russian fur hunters seek sea otters along the outer Pacific coast. Several Tlingit stories tell of a fleet of Indian canoes which capsize at the entrance to Lituya Bay. Their harvest of furs in watertight skin bags drift to the Russian far east, luring Russian fur traders.

1778 • Captain James Cook of the British *Resolution* names Mt. Fairweather and locates Dry Bay on the park's northwest corner. The crew includes George Vancouver and William Bligh (of *Mutiny on the Bounty* fame). Cook obtains sea otter pelts from Alaska Natives and sells them at handsome prices to the Chinese, spurring a rush of fur trading expeditions to Southeast Alaska.

1786 • French explorer Jean Francois Galoup de La Perouse enters Lituya Bay. He describes the head of Lituya Bay as "perhaps the most extraordinary place in the world." He is the first-known white man to land on the outer coast of what is now the park. He

KEY: The historical photographs are courtesy of the following institutions and identified by their prefix and collection number:
ASL: Alaska State Library, Historical Collections
GBNP: Glacier Bay National Park and Preserve Photo Collection
LC: Library of Congress Collections
AMNH: American Museum of Natural History, Department of Library Services

purchases Cenotaph Island from Tlingits living in three seasonal villages in Lituya Bay and claims it for France. Twenty-one crewmen in small boats are lost in the strong tide at the bay's entrance. Known as the "jaws of death," the entrance claims at least 100 people during recorded history.

1788 • The Russian galiot *Three Saints* departs the Russian settlement at Kodiak to explore the American mainland. Navigators Izmailov and Bocharov visit the Tlingit village at Yakutat then enter Lituya Bay on July 3. They trade with the Indians at the summer camp and acquire the broken anchor left by the French two years before. Tlingit oral tradition recounts the first encounters with the French (in 1786) and the Russians.

1794 • Captain George Vancouver of the *Discovery* continues Captain Cook's search for the northwest passage. Vancouver describes the mouth of Glacier Bay, a mere five mile indentation in the coastline, as blocked by "compact and solid mountains of ice, rising perpendicular from the waters edge."

1799 • Baranof establishes Sitka as a white settlement and capital of Russian America. Excessive hunting depletes the sea otters and enrages the Tlingits, who attack the new Russian forts in Sitka in 1802 and Yakutat in 1805.

1867 • William Henry Seward, Secretary of State, purchases Alaska from Russia for $7,200,000. The deal draws criticism from the press and is ridiculed as "Seward's Folly" and "Seward's Icebox." The *New York World* declares "Russia has sold us a sucked orange," referring to the fast-disappearing sea otters.

1877 • American Lt. Charles Woods briefly explores the ice-filled Glacier Bay, probably leading the first party of white explorers to do so.

1878 • William Henry Dall of the U.S. Coast Survey names the point of land at the eastern entrance to Glacier Bay for King Gustavus II of Sweden. For many years, the area is known as Strawberry Point. Now it is Gustavus.

1879 • Naturalist and writer John Muir explores Glacier Bay, seeking first-hand experience of glaciers. He is an early proponent of the theory that glaciers once covered the North American continent. He travels in a dugout canoe in October, crewed by Tlingit Indians from Wrangell; Toyatte, a Stickeen nobleman, leads the group. S. Hall Young, a Presbyterian missionary, accompanies Muir. The glacial ice has retreated 40 miles from where Vancouver's party saw it. They spend five days mapping and naming features in the bay. The *San Francisco Bulletin* prints Muir's vivid descriptions of the area, which sparks the interest of scientists, explorers and tourists.

Native settlement at Dundas Bay ASL PCA 39-637

Hoonah Chief "Nah-Kane" ASL PCA 39-406

Jean-François de Galaup de LaPerouse ASL PCA 20-242

Village of Hoonah ASL PCA 39-405

John Muir, c.1902 LC USZ62-52000 914816

Muir Cabin at Muir Inlet, 1890 GBNP #4339

Steamer *City of Topeka*, c.1895 ASL PCA 87-1733

1880 • Muir and Young return to visit Taylor Bay, Dundas Bay and Muir Glacier. Tyeen, a Tlingit Indian from Wrangell, guides the party. Young's dog accompanies the expedition and shares a harrowing adventure with Muir, recounted in his book, *Stickeen: The Story of a Dog.*

1880 • Captain Lester S. Beardslee, US Navy, names Glacier Bay.

1883 • James Carroll, captain of the Pacific Coast Steamship Company's *Idaho,* pilots the first tourists into the Glacier Bay. Carroll names the bay's largest glacier and its inlet for John Muir. Passenger Eliza Scidmore describes her adventures for New York and St. Louis newspapers and eventually writes the first tour guide for Southeast Alaska.

1890 • Muir makes his third visit to Glacier Bay. He constructs a cabin a half mile from the face of Muir Glacier, now known as Muir Point. He and another team of scientists led by Harry Reid build stone cairns to mark glacial activity, key reference points for future researchers.

1890-99 • Placer miners work the ruby-colored sands of Lituya Bay for powder-fine gold. 1896 is the banner year, employing up to 200 men. Intermittent activity continues into the 1930s.

1898 • The Klondike Gold Rush is underway in Alaska and the Yukon.

1899 • The Harriman Alaska Expedition, organized and funded by railroad tycoon Edward Harriman, visits Glacier Bay and Lituya Bay during a two-month survey of coastal Alaska. In addition to John Muir, the prominent group includes 24 scientists, three artists and two photographers.

1899 • In September, an earthquake in Yakutat Bay, measuring 8.4 on the Richter scale, causes heavy ice calving in Glacier Bay. Ships can no longer navigate the ice-choked bays, bringing tourism and scientific expeditions to a halt. Since 1893, 25,000 tourists have visited the bay by steamer.

1899 • At a camp north of Lituya Bay, five gold miners are stranded by bad weather for the winter. One of the prospectors, Martin Severts, shoots two men, killing one of them. But he is overpowered by the married couple before he can kill them and steal the group's $800 poke of gold dust. Unable to send the man out to Juneau or Sitka nor to guard him for the rest of the winter, Edith and Hans Nelson try him, find him guilty and hang him. The place bears the name Justice Creek. Jack London recounts the adventure in his short story "The Unexpected."

1914 • Three young married couples attempt the first homesteading at Strawberry Point, now Gustavus. The Henry, Taggart and Davis families jointly build their first log building, dubbing it the Honeymoon Ranch. That fall, they celebrate Saturday nights by dressing up in their gayest clothes, cranking up the gramophone, and dancing to the popular tune, "All Dressed Up and No Place to Go." Discouraged by the difficult frontier conditions, the families eventually move south.

1917 • Abraham Lincoln Parker and his family start a homestead near Gustavus Point. A.L. Parker works his newly purchased horse to plow his first fields, which are circular. He later learns the horse was trained for the circus tent. The extended Parker family earns patents on five homesteads and raises cattle, runs a sawmill and mines gold in Reid Inlet. They construct some of the first roads, bridges, docks and buildings in the community.

1917 • James Huscroft settles on Cenotaph Island in Lituya Bay, trapping and silver fox farming. For many years, he is the sole inhabitant of the bay and the 155 mile-long coastline from Cape Spencer to Yakutat. Although a hermit, he is famous for his hospitality, and he houses visitors in a log bunkhouse called "Huscroft Hotel." Every year, Huscroft makes the 155 mile trip to Juneau by rowboat. He picks up supplies and a year's worth of newspapers, which he reads, one a day, exactly a year late.

1922 • William Cooper, a scientist who first studies the area in 1916, successfully urges the Ecological Society of America to support making Glacier Bay a nationally protected site. The next year, the society proposes the bay for park or monument status, noting that the area is a natural laboratory for scientific analysis.

1925 • President Calvin Coolidge establishes Glacier Bay National Monument on February 26. Hoonah Tlingit Indians, fox farmers, miners, Gustavus homesteaders, and other Southeast Alaska business interests oppose the restrictions of a monument.

1925 • A lighthouse at Cape Spencer begins operation, manned by a crew of four, and signaling the entrance to Cross Sound. The facility is automated in 1974.

1930 • Members of the Harvard-Dartmouth Alaska Expedition led by Bradford Washburn attempt the first of several assents in the Fairweather Range. They return four more times and climb Mt. Crillon in 1934 and Mount Bertha in 1940.

1931 • Allen Carpe' and Terris Moore scale Mt. Fairweather for the first time. Fellow climbers William Ladd and Andrew Taylor voluntarily descend to a lower camp when dwindling food supplies could feed only two men.

1936 • The International Boundary Commission settles a century-old dispute between the U.S. and Canada over the location of their border in Southeast Alaska. The boundary is drawn through the Grand Pacific Glacier, placing Glacier Bay in U.S. territory.

1936 • Congress and President Franklin Roosevelt open Glacier Bay Monument to mining, persuaded in part by novelist Rex Beach, working on behalf of his friends, Joe and Muz Ibach. Through the mid-1950s, the Ibachs stake and work various claims, notably at Reid Inlet.

1939 • Glacier Bay National Monument doubles in size through a proclamation by President Roosevelt. Public concern for protecting brown bear habitat is a key factor. Homesteaders at Gustavus protest the addition of their site to the monument. Dundas Bay, Excursion Inlet and the Fairweather Coast are also incorporated.

Early 1940s • The Gustavus Point airfield is built to support WWII efforts in the Aleutian Islands.

Muir Glacier from 1800 feet, 1893   GBNP #3826

Jim Huscroft and Ernie Rognan, Lituya Bay, c.1932   GBNP#4380

Henry, Taggart and Davis family settlers in Gustavus, 1914   GBNP #5931

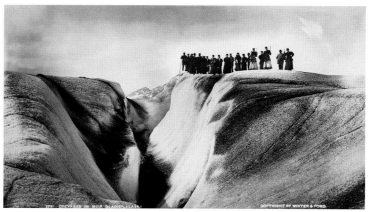

Muir Glacier and tourists, 1895   ASL PCA 87-2031

POW Camp, Excursion Inlet, 1945

ASL PCA 175-116

Glacier Bay naturalist on tour ship

GBNP #5968

Overnight boat bow lands between Margerie and Grand Pacific Glacier in the early 1980s.

©1982 Mark Kelley

1943 • The U.S. Army completes construction of a secret shipping base at Excursion Inlet, on land transferred from the monument. The $17 million facility is built to stockpile supplies for a U.S. operation to reclaim two Aleutian Islands, then occupied by the Japanese. The Japanese are driven off the islands before the facility is completed. German prisoners-of-war spend half a year dismantling the "white elephant" in 1945.

1946 • Hoonah Tlingits' use of Glacier Bay for subsistence and commercial gathering is documented in a report for the Bureau of Indian Affairs. The report lists seal, goat and marmot hunting, gull egg collecting, berry picking, trapping, catching and smoking salmon. The researchers gather the information to address increasing controversy over the Indians' use of Glacier Bay resources.

1954 • Gustavus homesteader and part-time resident Charlie Parker mounts a letter-writing campaign to convince Alaska newspaper editors and officials in Washington, DC that Gustavus should be excluded from the Glacier Bay National Monument. The airport and forelands and part of Excursion Inlet are removed from the monument by President Dwight Eisenhower in 1955.

1958 • An enormous deposit of copper-nickel is discovered in the bedrock beneath the Brady Icefield. By 1971, developers propose a three-mile tunnel under the glacier, a 13-mile road and a mill at Dixon Harbor on the outer coast of the monument.

1958 • An earthquake measuring 8.0 along a fault line under the Fairweather Mountains produces massive rock and snow slides at the upper end of Lituya Bay. They trigger a gigantic wave that climbs 1,720 feet high up a nearby slope, a height 470 feet taller than the Empire State Building. The displaced water rips trees, rocks and soil from five square miles of the bay's shoreline and engulfs three fishing boats. The *FV Edrie* rides out the succeeding waves; but the *FV Sunmore* is lost as it attempts the bay's entrance. The giant wave carries the *FV Badger* 80 feet above the trees of the spit and into the ocean; the owners, the Swansons, escape in their dingy. In total, five lives and two boats are lost.

1966 • Glacier Bay Lodge is built at Bartlett Cove, the location chosen because of its proximity to the Gustavus Airstrip. Exactly 50 years after his first plant succession research trip to the area, ecologist William Cooper speaks at the dedication of the lodge.

1968 • About four dozen sea otters from the Aleutian Islands are released near Cape Spencer, in an attempt to reintroduce the mammals to Glacier Bay. After more transplants, otters are thriving along the outside coast, in Icy Strait and in the Beardslee Islands.

1969 • In the fall, the cruise ship *Mariposa* sails up the bay. The following year, more cruise ships add Glacier Bay to their itinerary, and 15,000 people visit the monument.

1974 • Hoonah's Tlingit Indians lose their aboriginal hunting privileges in Glacier Bay. An agreement dating from 1939 is rescinded.

1980 • The Alaska National Interest Lands Conservation Act makes Glacier Bay a national park, now covering 3.2 million acres. President Jimmy Carter signs the bill that adds 585,000 acres, over the objections of Alaska's three members of Congress. Mining is halted and more than 80 percent of the park—called the back country—is designated wilderness, with motorized access and commercial fishing prohibited. The 57,800 acres of the Alsek River area are designated as preserve, allowing sport hunting and commercial fishing to continue.

1981 • Some 86,850 people visit Glacier Bay National Park; 80 percent of them arrive by cruise ships.

1981 • A black bear kills and eats a kayaker at Sandy Cove. The cove is closed to back country use for the rest of the season. In later years, the National Park Service works to avoid people-bear encounters by experimenting with bear-proof food containers and orienting all back country visitors to clean camping.

1984 • A decline in the number of humpback whales feeding and summering in the bay prompts the Park Service to regulate cruise ship and tour boat traffic. The federal government had listed the humpback whale as an endangered species in 1969.

1986 • Glacier Bay National Park, along with Admiralty Island National Monument, is designated an International Biosphere Reserve by the United Nations.

1992 • The number of tourists visiting Glacier Bay increases to 216,829. Seventy-seven percent are cruise ship and tour boat passengers.

1992 • Glacier Bay National Park and Preserve is named part of a U.S. / Canada World Heritage Site. Including the Wrangell-St. Elias National Park in Alaska, and the Kluane National Park Reserve and the Tatshenshini-Alsek Wilderness Provincial Park in Canada, the World Heritage Site encompasses 24 million acres. It is the largest internationally protected area in the world. The new status helps halt development of a proposed gigantic open pit copper mine on the Tatshenshini River in Canada.

1996 • Goldbelt, Incorporated, a Juneau Native corporation, takes over the operation of the Glacier Bay Lodge, charter and tour operations.

1997 • Proposed regulations phase out commercial fishing from the bay over a 15-year period.

1997 • Park visitors total 336,226 for the season. Of those people, 306,216 book passage on cruise ships, and 25,419 are passengers on the smaller tour boats. The National Park Service limits the number of vessels in park waters on a daily basis: two cruise ships, three tour boats, six charter boats and 25 private boats.

1998 • The Mt. Fairweather Golf Course opens in Gustavus. The 9-hole course is located on the DeBoer Family's 1959 homestead and on uplifted land created as the glaciers recede.

Glacier Bay day boat cruises in front of Riggs Glacier in 1980. ©1980 Mark Kelley

Dining room in Park Hotel © 1998 Mark Kelley

Trail marker along Bartlett Cove hiking trail carved in 1998. ©1998 Mark Kelley

▲ Young anglers measure themselves against their 45-pound halibut caught in Glacier Bay. The record catch for the State of Alaska is 459 pounds and the largest halibut caught in the waters surrounding Glacier Bay weighed in at 440 pounds.

Fascinating Facts About Glacier Bay

▲ **Mt. Fairweather**

Glacier Bay National Park and Preserve covers 3,280,000 acres: 3,271,000 acres in the park and 57,000 acres in the preserve.

▲▲▲

Approximately 2.7 million acres of the park and preserve, about 80 percent, are designated as wilderness under the Wilderness Act.

▲▲▲

Glacier Bay is the world's largest protected marine sanctuary.

▲▲▲

Mount Fairweather towers over the park at 15,320 feet. The Alaska-Canada border crosses through its peak.

▲▲▲

Glacier Bay is slightly larger than the state of Connecticut (third smallest in the U.S.), but contains less than one percent of Alaska's land mass.

▲▲▲

Although taller than any mountain in the other 49 states, Mount Fairweather ranks only 19 among Alaska's towering peaks. In Europe, only Mount Blanc in France is higher than Mount Fairweather—and by just 471 feet.

Mount Fairweather's neighboring peaks are Mount Quincy Adams (13,650 ft), Mount Crillon (12,728 ft), Mount Root (12,860 ft), Mount Salisbury (12,000 ft), Mount Lituya (11,924 ft), La Perouse (10,728 ft), Mount Lodge (10,530 ft) and Mount Bertha (10,000 ft).

▲▲▲

During the Great Ice Age (the Pleistocene), an immense sheet of ice 5,000 feet thick covered Southeastern and Southcentral Alaska, advancing and receding at least four times. The most recent advance is known as the Little Ice Age and occurred from 1500 AD until the late 18th century.

▲▲▲

In Gustavus, land that was formerly underwater is rising out of the ocean at a rate of more than an inch a year. Glaciers' enormous bulk weighs down the land; as the ice recedes, the land rises.

▲▲▲

Glaciers abound in the park and preserve: 16 tidewater glaciers, 30 valley or alpine glaciers and a dozen smaller, unnamed glaciers.

The path of the giant wave from the 1958 earthquake in Lituya Bay reached a height of 1,720 feet.

▲▲▲

The Tlingit Indians call the area Sitadaka, and the word survives in the name of Sitakaday Narrows, at the mouth of Glacier Bay.

▲▲▲

Ice calving into Glacier Bay is an average of 200 years old.

▲▲▲

La Perouse Glacier is the only glacier on the continental U.S. that flows directly into the Pacific Ocean.

▲▲▲

Glacier Bay is a living laboratory for the study of plant succession. The retreat of the glaciers began 200 years ago, and the vegetation displays two centuries of succeeding growth, from barren moraine at a glacier's terminus to mature coastal forest at Bartlett Cove.

▲▲▲

Five major earthquakes, triggered along the Fairweather-Queen Charlotte Fault paralleling the outer coast, have been recorded in the past 150 years: 1853, 1874, 1899, 1936 and 1958.

Mount Fairweather's peak is only 15 miles from the coast, rising abruptly from the Pacific Ocean. The rise averages 1,000 feet per mile.

▲▲▲

The Tlingit name for Mount Fairweather was "Tanaku." Reportedly, Tlingits used the mountain to "read" weather conditions along the coast; they would not leave sheltered water unless they could see the mountain's peak.

▲▲▲

The retreat of Glacier Bay's rivers of ice, since Captain Vancouver's sighting in 1796, is the fastest known anywhere in the world.

▲▲▲

The color of glacial ice is varied. White ice contains trapped air bubbles; deep blue signals dense, compacted ice. Greenish-black ice comes from the bottom of a glacier; while brown and black ice contains rocks fallen from the mountain cliffs along the glacier's track.

▲▲▲

In 1998, some 339,000 passengers visited Glacier Bay on cruise ships. An additional 19,700 people toured the bay on mid-size tour boats.

Fish & Crab
of Glacier Bay

*The species listed below are a few of the common species
of fish and crab that inhabit Glacier Bay.*

Chum salmon
Coho salmon
Cutthroat trout
Dolly Varden char
Dungeness crab
Eulachon
Gray cod
Halibut
Hermit crab
Kelp crab
Kelp greenling
King crab
King salmon
Ling cod
Mud shark
Pink salmon
Rockfish
Sculpin
Shrimp
Skate
Sockeye salmon
Starry flounder
Steelhead trout
Stickleback
Tanner crab

▲ **Harvest of shrimp**

◀ **King crab**

▲ **White and pink lupine with purple lupine in background**

► **Lupine along Salmon River in Gustavus**

Common Plant Families of Glacier Bay

Adder's tongue fern
Bracken
Club moss
Cypress
Deer fern
Horsetail
Lady fern
Maidenhair
Marsh fern
Pine
Quillwort
Shield fern
Spikemoss

Flowering Plants

Arrow grass
Arum *(Yellow skunk cabbage)*
Beach greens
Birch
Bladderwort
Bluebell
Blueberry
Borage
Broomrape
Buckwheat
Bur reed
Crowberry
Crowfoot *(Marsh marigold)*
Dogwood *(Dwarf dogwood)*
Dwarf fireweed
False lily-of-the-valley
Figwort *(Indian Paintbrush)*
Fireweed
Gentian
Gingseng *(Devil's club)*
Goosefoot
Geranium
Grass

Heath *(Bearberry)*
Honeysuckle
Iris
Jewelweed
Lily *(Chocolate lily)*
Lupine
Madder
Mint
Mistletoe
Nettle
Oleaster
Orchid *(Coral root)*
Parsley
Pea
Pink
Plantain
Polemonium or Phlox
Pondweed
Poppy
Primrose *(Shooting star)*
Purslane
Rose
Rush
Sandalwood
Saxifrage *(Trailing black currant)*
Sedge *(Alaska cotton)*
Stonecrop
Sundew
Sunflower
Valerian
Violet
Waterleaf
Water lily *(Yellow pond lily)*
Water milfoil
Water starwort
Wax myrtle
Willow
Wintergreen

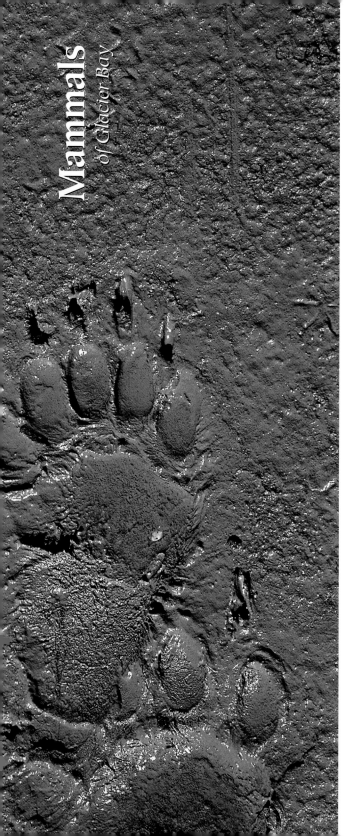

Mammals of Glacier Bay

The mammals listed below range from very common to very rare. The varying habitats of Glacier Bay contribute to a patchy distribution of many of these species.

Beaver
Black bear
Brown bear
Coyote
Dall porpoise
Deer mouse
Finback whale
Gray whale
Harbor porpoise
Harbor seal
Hoary marmot
Humpback whale
Little brown bat
Least weasel
Longtail vole
Lynx
Marten
Masked shrew
Mink
Minke whale
Moose
Mountain goat
Northern fur seal
Northern flying squirrel
Northern water shrew
Orca
Porcupine
Redback vole
Red fox
Red squirrel
River otter
Sea otter
Short-tailed weasel
Sitka blacktailed deer
Snowshoe hare
Steller sea lion
Tundra vole
Wandering shrew
Wolf
Wolverine

▲ **Black bear**
◀ **Black bear print in tidal mud**

◀ **Seagull nest**

▶ **Seagulls at nest along Muir Inlet**

Birds of Glacier Bay

There are 223 bird species found to date within Glacier Bay National Park and Preserve. Listed below are some of the more common species.

American robin
American wigeon
Arctic loon
Arctic tern
Bald eagle
Barn swallow
Barrow's goldeneye
Black-billed magpie
Black-legged kittiwake
Black oystercatcher
Blue grouse
Bonaparte's gull
Bufflehead
Canada goose
Common loon
Common murre
Common merganser
Common raven
Dark-eyed junco
Dunlin
Fox sparrow
Glaucous-winged gull
Golden-crowned sparrow
Greater yellowlegs
Green-winged teal
Harlequin duck
Hermit thrush

Least sandpiper
Kittlitz's murrelet
Mallard
Marbled murrelet
Mew gull
Northern phalarope
Northwestern crow
Oldsquaw
Orange-crowned warbler
Pacific loon
Pelagic cormorant
Pigeon guillemot
Pine siskin
Red-breasted merganser
Red-necked phalarope
Red-throated loon
Ruby-crowned kinglet
Savannah sparrow
Spotted sandpiper
Surf scoter
Tree swallow
Tufted puffin
Varied thrush
Western sandpiper
White winged scoter
Wilson's warbler

Photo by Joe Geifer

MARK KELLEY

Mark Kelley, 46, of Juneau, Alaska has been a freelance photographer for more than 20 years. His photos have appeared on the covers of more than 100 publications including Alaska and national magazines, books, brochures, calendars and annual reports. *Glacier Bay National Park: Alaska* is Mark's sixth book of photos. He also publishes calendars of Juneau and Southeast Alaska and a line of 44 note cards.

Mark was born and raised in Buffalo, N.Y. He moved to Alaska in 1974 to attend the University of Alaska Fairbanks. Graduating in 1978 with a degree in journalism and northern studies, he worked for a year for the *Ithaca Journal* in New York before returning to Alaska in 1979. He worked as a newspaper photojournalist at the *Juneau Empire* for 14 years until he left in 1993 to freelance full-time. Mark also did graduate studies in photojournalism at Ohio University in Athens.

Mark lives in Juneau with his wife and two sons. He and his family are avid outdoors people, especially enjoying soccer, skiing, sportfishing and camping.

SHERRY SIMPSON

Sherry Simpson grew up in Juneau and lives with her husband in Fairbanks, where she teaches journalism at the University of Alaska Fairbanks. She is the author of *The Way Winter Comes*, a book of essays about Alaska that won the 1998 Chinook Literary Prize.

PHOTOGRAPHER'S NOTES

My first trip to Glacier Bay was in the summer of 1980. Over the intervening years, I've been fortunate to return often—but never enough. During the past two years, I spent more than 11 weeks in the park shooting most of the photos in this book.

The more time I spend in the park, the more I realize just how much there is—and how little of it I've really seen. Keeping that in mind, I look forward to a lifetime of my annual explorations and discoveries in the park.

Whether you are on a day cruise or a three-week kayak trip, I hope this book gives you a better appreciation of the park's enormous potential and instills in you a desire to protect that potential for all generations. I want my children's children to revel in the same spirit of adventure and wilderness that I enjoy.

The wildlife photos were all shot with a telephoto lens with a minimum 300mm. The animals were photographed with great care and concern for their welfare, and I always had a companion for added safety.

In respect for the park's restriction on approaching wildlife, most but not all of the photos were taken in the park or preserve. Some of the other photos were taken in the waters adjacent to the park. Because of the need to protect sensitive wildlife areas, not all photos are clearly identified with a place name.

I shot the photographs in this book using Nikon cameras and lenses. I used F5 camera bodies and a wide range of lenses including: 20mm to 35mm zoom, 35mm to 75mm zoom, 80mm to 200mm zoom, 100mm macro, 300mm and 500mm. Most of the photos were shot on Velvia film and processed at Front Street Photo in Juneau, with a few Kodachrome images included from my early years in the park. I used graduated neutral-density filters and polarizing filters. None of the photos in this book have been digitally retouched or manipulated.

Mark Kelley
Juneau, Alaska
September 1999

▲ **Lituya Bay**

▲ Black-legged kittiwakes

ACKNOWLEDGMENTS

The creation of a book takes the hard work and good will of many people.

For their help in making this book financially possible, while enthusiastically supporting the whole concept from day one, I thank Goldbelt, Incorporated and its Board of Directors. Specifically, I appreciate the efforts of Joe Beedle, Margaret Nelson, Susan Bell, Todd Antioquia, Paula Cadiente and board members Alberta Aspen, Andrea Cadiente-Laiti, Del Cesar, Joe Kahklen, Robert Martin Jr., Edith McHenry, Carl Nelson, Kathy Polk, Randy Wanamaker and Dorothy Zura.

For helping me along the way by giving me a dry place to crash or a good meal, by carrying some of my load, by just keeping me company on the long wet days, by driving and paddling the boats or by sharing the success of a good day, I thank Paul Johnson and Tami Mullick from Gull Cove Lodge; Joe Giefer from Admiralty Island Wilderness Homestead; Bobo Bell, Brian Beauchamp, Brien Daugherty, Monte Paulsen, Gary Gray from Alsek River Lodge; Koren and Rob Bosworth, Meadow Brook and Chris Smith from Meadow's Glacier Bay Guest House; Steve and Deborah Hemenway from Shearwater Lodge; Richard Steele, Hank Lentfer, and Bob and Elaine Schroeder.

For making their trips available to me, thanks goes to Alaska Discovery including Ken Leghorn, Sue Warner, Barb Kelly, John Scheerens and the Discovery guides Sierra Kaden, Jeff Sloss, Amy Reifenstein and Ken McGowan.

For listening and providing advice, thanks to Glacier Bay National Park superintendents Tomie Lee and Jim Brady, national park staff Randy King, Mary Beth Moss and Caroline Elder; Friends of Glacier Bay Kim Heacox, Bill Brown and Hank Lentfer and Hoonah Indian Association Kenneth Grant and Maureen Brown.

For their help in keeping this book on its production schedule, I appreciate the efforts of my assistant and historical researcher, Odette Foster; the writer, Sherry Simpson; the book designer, Laura Lucas; word editors, Larry Persily and Tricia Brown; and digital wizard, Eric Torgerson from Catchlight Digital Imaging.

For assistance with historical research and photographs, thanks to the staff of the Alaska State Library Historical Collections in Juneau.

For processing all of the hundreds of rolls of slides to make my schedule, thanks to Front Street Photo including Duane, Eileen and Gerrit Plate.

For explaining the plight of the black-legged kittiwakes, thanks goes to Elizabeth Ross Hooge.

For letting me use a photo I shot for Sealaska, thanks goes to Sealaska Corporation and Ross Soboleff.

For help in production and printing of this book, I thank my friends at Samwha Printing Company including Mimi Lee, Willy Lee, Anthony Cho; and also Flip Todd and Tina Wallace from Todd Communications.

Finally, thanks to my wife, Jan, and my boys, Gabe and Owen, for all their love, support and the fun they bring to my life.

Mark Kelley
September 1999